INVESTIGA

PLANTS

SUPER COOL SCIENCE EXPERIMENTS

CHERRY LAKE PRESS
Ann Arbor, Michigan

by Susan H. Gray

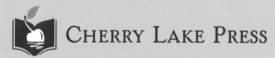

CHERRY LAKE PRESS

Published in the United States of America by
Cherry Lake Publishing Group
Ann Arbor, Michigan
www.cherrylakepublishing.com

Reading Adviser: Beth Walker Gambro, MS, Ed., Reading Consultant, Yorkville, IL

Content Editor: Robert Wolffe, EdD,
Professor of Teacher Education, Bradley University, Peoria, Illinois

Book Designer: Ed Morgan of Bowerbird Books

Grateful acknowledgment to Deborah Simon, Department of Chemistry,
Whitman College

Photo Credits: cover and title page, 4, 6, 7, 8, 12, 16, 20, 23, 24, 27, 28, 29, freepik.com; 5, 9, 10, 11, 13, 14, 15, 17, 18, 19, 21, 22, 25, 26, The Design Lab.

Cherry Lake Press is an imprint of Cherry Lake Publishing Group.

Library of Congress Cataloging-in-Publication Data has been filed and is available at
catalog.loc.gov

Printed in the United States of America
Corporate Graphics

A Note to Parents and Teachers: Please review the instructions for these experiments before your children do them. Be sure to help them with any experiments you do not think they can safely conduct on their own.

A Note to Kids: Be sure to ask an adult for help with these experiments when you need it. Always put your safety first!

Note from Publisher: Websites change regularly, and their future contents are outside of our control.
Supervise children when conducting any recommended online searches for extended learning opportunities.

CONTENTS

Amazing
PLANTS

Look outside. Do you see anything with green leaves, bark, or flowers? There are often a variety of plants in the places where we live. Plants don't just make Earth more beautiful. They serve an important purpose. Plants make **oxygen** that people breathe. Also, much of the food we eat, such as vegetables, nuts, and seeds, comes from plants. On top of that, plants give us shelter. We build homes from wood. And trees provide much-needed shade from the Sun.

Nearly 30 percent of Earth's oxygen is produced by trees.

OXYGEN

Getting
STARTED

We can take an even closer look at plants using science! Scientists learn about plants by studying them. They do this by thinking clearly, asking questions, and carrying out experiments. They write down their **observations** and their discoveries, which often leads to new questions and experiments. In this book, we'll learn how to think and act like real scientists. You'll also design your own experiments using supplies you may already have at home!

SCIENCE NOTES

When scientists design experiments, they often use the scientific method. What is the scientific method? It's a step-by-step process to answer specific questions. The steps don't always follow the same pattern. However, the scientific method often works like this:

STEP ONE: A scientist gathers the facts and makes observations about one particular thing.

STEP TWO: The scientist comes up with a question that is not answered by the observations and facts.

STEP THREE: The scientist creates a **hypothesis**. This is a statement about what the scientist thinks might be the answer to the question.

STEP FOUR: The scientist tests the hypothesis by designing an experiment to see whether the hypothesis is correct. Then the scientist carries out the experiment and writes down what happens.

STEP FIVE: The scientist draws a **conclusion** based on the result of the experiment. The conclusion might be that the hypothesis is correct. Sometimes, though, the hypothesis is not correct. In that case, the scientist might develop a new hypothesis and another experiment.

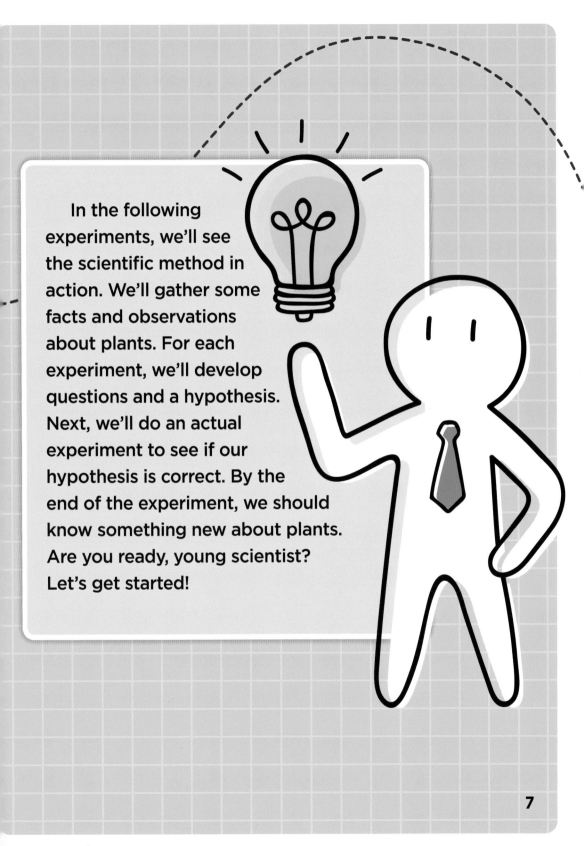

In the following experiments, we'll see the scientific method in action. We'll gather some facts and observations about plants. For each experiment, we'll develop questions and a hypothesis. Next, we'll do an actual experiment to see if our hypothesis is correct. By the end of the experiment, we should know something new about plants. Are you ready, young scientist? Let's get started!

· EXPERIMENT 1 ·

Roots and Shoots

Think about the things you already know about plants. There's a good chance you know that many plants grow from seeds. Soon after they are planted and watered, something amazing happens. They **germinate**, or begin to grow! During germination, the roots and stem both grow from the seed. But which grows first? If the roots grow first, they could anchor the plant. Then the stem and leaves can grow upright.

Let's do an experiment to see if the roots grow first. Come up with a hypothesis. Here's one option: **The roots of bean seeds will begin to grow before the stems do.**

Here's what you'll need:

- A marker
- 4 clear plastic cups, each with 3 holes punched into the bottom. Ask an adult to help you make the holes.
- 4 different kinds of bean seeds. You can use dried lima beans, great northern beans, pinto beans, red beans, or kidney beans. You can find these at a grocery store or garden center.
- Potting soil
- Saucers or trays for the cups to sit in
- Water
- A warm spot, such as a sunny windowsill

· INSTRUCTIONS ·

1. Use a marker to label the cups with the names of the 4 different kinds of beans.

2. Fill the cups with potting soil.

3. In each cup, plant 4 of the same type of bean. Plant them about 1 inch (2.5 centimeters) deep. Place the beans close to the sides of the cup. This way, you can watch the seeds as they germinate.

4. Place the cups on saucers or trays.

5. Water the seeds and set the cups in a warm spot.

6. For the rest of the experiment, keep the soil moist but not soaking wet.

7. Look at the plants every day until the shoots have grown about 1 inch (2.5 cm) above the soil. Write down your observations each day. Pay attention to which part of each plant grows first. Is it the roots or the stem?

· CONCLUSION ·

What did you learn from this experiment? How many plants grew roots first? How many sprouted a stem first? Was your hypothesis correct? Was the hypothesis correct for all four of the plants?

FACTS!

Roots grow first to help plants take in water. They also anchor the plant. It makes sense that roots would begin to grow before stems. So what's the point of testing this idea? Good scientists know that they can't always believe something that seems to make sense. Experiments help prove what's actually true.

· EXPERIMENT 2 ·

Light Versus Dark

All living things need energy to live and grow. Plants get their energy from sunlight. But how much sunlight do plants need to survive? That's a question a **botanist** might ask. It's also an interesting question for us to explore. Let's develop another hypothesis and experiment using bean plants. Here's one possibility: **Bean plants grow best when they have sunlight all day long.**

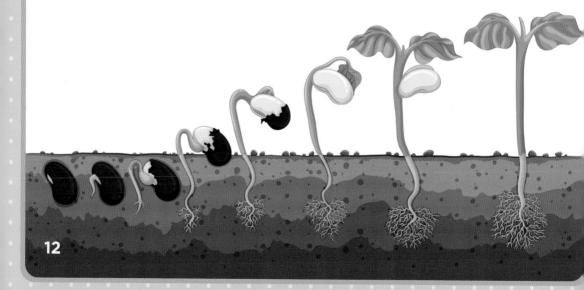

Here's what you'll need:

- A marker
- 4 small bean plants (Grow the plants the same way you did in the last experiment. Start with cups with three holes punched into the bottom and fill with potting soil. Plant seeds in each. Grow just one type of bean. The plants should be no more than 2 inches (5.1 cm) tall.)
- 4 saucers or trays for the cups to sit in
- A warm, sunny spot such as a windowsill
- 3 tall, empty boxes or coffee cans that are big enough to cover the cups

· INSTRUCTIONS ·

1. Use the marker to label the cups "0 hours," "1 hour," "2 hours," and "all day."

2. Place the cups on the saucers or trays and put them in a sunny spot.

3. Use the boxes or coffee cans to cover all of the cups except the "all day" cup.

4. For the next 10 days, keep the "0 hours" cup covered except when you water it. Water each plant every 3 days to keep the soil moist throughout the experiment.

5. Uncover the "1 hour" cup for only 1 hour each day. Uncover the "2 hours" cup for 2 hours each day. Let the "all day" cup remain uncovered.

6. Write down what you see happening to the plants each day.

· CONCLUSION ·

Which plants seem to be the healthiest after 10 days? Which ones look the sickest? How can you tell? Look at the color of the leaves. How green are they? How yellow? Which plants are the tallest? Do you think the tallest plants are the healthiest ones? Was your hypothesis correct?

FACTS!

When scientists do experiments, they must consider **variables**. Variables are things that affect how experiments turn out. Heat, moisture, sunlight, and pollution are some variables that can affect plant growth. In this simple experiment, only one variable changed—the amount of sunlight the plants received. Everything else stayed the same, such as the type of plants used, the position of the plants, how warm they were, and so on. If too many variables change during an experiment, it can be very hard to draw a conclusion.

15

· EXPERIMENT 3 ·

Is Green Always Best?

Sunlight is made up of different colors. If you've ever seen light that has passed through a **prism**, you may already know this. You may also have seen these seven colors—red, orange, yellow, green, blue, indigo (deep bluish purple), and violet—in a rainbow.

Plants need sunlight to grow. But do you think plants use all seven colors of sunlight? And do plants grow better in certain colors? Let's develop a hypothesis: **Because plants are green, they will grow best in green light.**

Here's what you'll need:

- 3 clear, 2-liter plastic soda bottles with the top 4 inches (10.2 cm) cut off (Ask an adult to help you with this.)
- Sheets of deeply colored cellophane. Use 2 different colors of the sun's light, such as red or blue. Do not use green. You might be able to find colored cellophane at a flower shop or craft store.
- 1 green, 2-liter plastic soda bottle with the top 4 inches (10.2 cm) cut off
- 4 small flowerpots filled with potting soil, each with 3 young bean plants just beginning to germinate
- A warm, sunny spot
- Scissors
- Tape

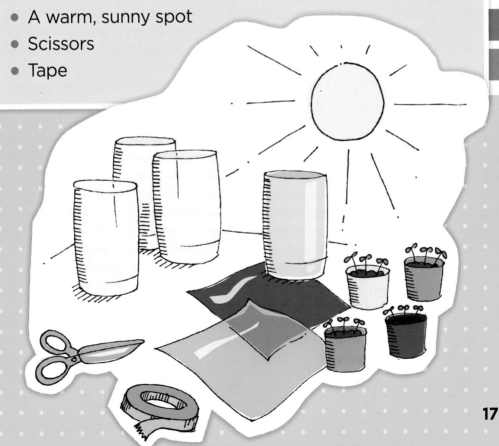

• INSTRUCTIONS •

1. Cover one of the clear bottles with sheets of one color of cellophane. Secure it with tape. Use the scissors to trim any extra cellophane. Make sure the bottle is completely covered. But do not cover the opening of the bottle.

2. Do the same with another clear bottle, using a different color of cellophane.

3. Leave one bottle clear. Do not cover the green bottle.

4. Set all 4 flowerpots in a warm, sunny spot. Cover each one with a soda bottle.

5. For the next 2 weeks, remove the bottles only long enough to quickly water the plants when the soil becomes too dry. Write down how the plants look every day.

CONCLUSION

After 2 weeks, which plants look the healthiest? Which ones look the sickest? Did the plants under the green bottle do the best? How can you tell? Was your hypothesis correct?

Scientists who study light probably could have predicted the results of this experiment. They know that all seven colors of light reach green plants. Those plants, however, absorb every color except green. The green light just bounces off. All seven colors of light also hit the green bottle. While some green light bounces off and some passes through, the bottle absorbs the other six colors. So the plants under the green bottle receive only green light. As a result, they get no energy from the green light. Does this help explain your results?

FACTS!

The very best scientists learn from other scientists and experts. What if we had asked an optics, or light, expert about how green light affects plants? How might their answer have affected our experiment? Maybe we would have come up with a completely different hypothesis to test!

· EXPERIMENT 4 ·

Cool Chlorophyll

Plants contain a green **pigment** called **chlorophyll**. Chlorophyll absorbs energy from sunlight along with **carbon dioxide** and water to create food for plants. Chlorophyll also gives plants their green color. Have you ever seen a plant that is not green? How about a sick or dying plant? What color are its leaves? What colors do some tree leaves turn in the autumn?

Could there be other pigments in green plants? Or is chlorophyll the only one? Let's find out. Come up with a hypothesis. Here are two possibilities:

Hypothesis #1: In addition to chlorophyll, there are other pigments in plant leaves.

Hypothesis #2: Chlorophyll is the only pigment in plant leaves.

Here's what you'll need:

- 3 fresh, green leaves. Maple, oak, and sweet gum tree leaves work great. Leaves from houseplants such as peace lilies and philodendrons also work well.
- A glass jar no more than 6 inches (15.2 cm) tall
- Rubbing alcohol (Alcohol will help to draw the pigments out of the leaves.)
- Water
- A small saucepan
- A stove (Ask an adult for help using the stove.)
- Scissors
- A coffee filter
- A pencil
- Tape

• INSTRUCTIONS •

1. Tear the leaves into small pieces and drop them into the jar.

2. Ask an adult for help with this step. Pour enough rubbing alcohol into the jar to cover the leaves. Be careful not to get the alcohol in your eyes or inhale its fumes.

3. Add about 1 inch (2.5 cm) of water to the saucepan. Have an adult heat the water on the stove. Let the water get very hot but not boiling.

4. Have the adult turn off the heat and remove the pan from the stove. Place the jar into the hot water in the saucepan. Let it remain there for about 30 minutes.

5. Use scissors to cut a strip of paper from the coffee filter. The strip should be about 1 inch (2.5 cm) wide and at least 6 inches (15.2 cm) long.

6. Rest a pencil across the top of the jar. Tape one end of the filter strip to the pencil so that the rest of the strip hangs down into the jar. The bottom of the strip should be just touching the alcohol.

7. Observe the filter paper as the alcohol creeps up it.

CONCLUSION

Look for any bands of color that appear on the strip. They may be very faint. It might be easier to see the colors if you remove the filter from the jar and let it dry. Did you see any colors other than green? What does this tell you? Was your hypothesis correct?

FACTS!

Some plants have pink, red, or orange leaves. They don't look like they contain chlorophyll, but they do! The color of the chlorophyll is masked by other darker pigments.

How Do Plants Absorb Water?

Plants need water to live. They use water to help build their stems, leaves, and other parts. But how does water travel to those tissues? Do the leaves of a plant soak up **moisture** from the air? Does water enter the plant roots? How exactly do plants absorb water? It's time for another experiment! Have you thought of a hypothesis? Try testing this one: **Plants draw water up their stems to their leaves.**

Here's what you'll need:

- Celery from the grocery store. Make sure several of the stalks have leaves.
- Ask an adult to help you select a small kitchen knife
- 2 glass jars
- Water
- Red or blue food coloring
- A warm, sunny spot
- A small spray bottle
- Some newspaper or paper towels

• INSTRUCTIONS •

1. Choose 2 of the celery stalks that have several leaves. Have an adult cut the stalks near the bottom.

2. Place one stalk with the cut end down in each glass jar.

3. Pour about 1 inch (2.5 cm) of water into one of the jars.

4. Add 6 drops of food coloring to the jar you just poured water into. Do not add water or food coloring to the other jar.

5. Place both jars in a warm, sunny spot.

6. Fill the spray bottle with water. Add 10 drops of food coloring to it.

7. For the next 4 hours, check on the stalks every 15 minutes. Each time you check them, take the stalk from the dry jar. Hold the stalk over the newspapers or

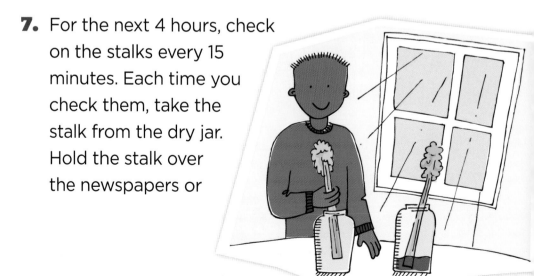

paper towels, and spray the leaves with the colored water. Let the water drip from the stalk onto the paper towels or newspapers. Then place it back in its jar.

8. At the end of 4 hours, gently rinse both stalks and their leaves.

CONCLUSION

How do the leaves look? What color are they? Now take the stalk of celery that sat in the colored water. Have an adult cut it in half. Look at where it was cut. See the tiny tubes? What color are they? What does that tell us about how leaves get their water? We used celery stalks without roots. In nature, the roots of a plant take in water. In many plants, the water is then carried through small tubes in the stem to the leaves. Was our hypothesis correct?

FACTS!

Florists use this trick to color flowers for special events. For example, someone might want a bright blue flower. But most flowers are not naturally blue. To create them, florists sometimes put white flowers in vases of blue-colored water!

Do It Yourself!

Picture a huge, glowing Moon and a field of corn. Some farmers believe that certain crops grow better when they are planted during a full Moon. For hundreds of years, they have been following this practice. Because farmers have been doing this for so long, does that mean it must be true? Or maybe the Moon has no effect on the crops.

The idea of growing plants based on the phases of the Moon is called Moon gardening.

The only way to know for sure is to do an experiment. So what would be your hypothesis? What materials would you need? How would you run the experiment? Don't forget your variables! How would you make sure that all plants were grown under the same conditions? How would you shield some plants from moonlight? How would you know if your "full Moon" plants grew better than the shielded plants?

FACTS!

Congratulations! You have just completed several experiments. Perhaps you'll use your new knowledge to grow the world's biggest beanstalk. Or maybe you'll create the first rainbow-colored carrots! Now that you can think like a scientist, so many things are possible!

Glossary

botanist (BOT-uh-nist) a scientist who studies plants

carbon dioxide (KAR-buhn dye-OK-side) a gas that is a mixture of carbon and oxygen

chlorophyll (KLOR-uh-fil) a green substance that gives green plants their color and uses light to produce food

conclusion (kuhn-KLOO-zhuhn) a final decision, thought, or opinion

germinate (JUR-muh-nate) to begin to grow roots and shoots

hypothesis (hye-POTH-uh-sihss) a logical guess of what will happen in an experiment

moisture (MOIS-chur) any form of water, including water vapor

observations (ob-zur-VAY-shuhnz) things that are seen or noticed with one's senses

oxygen (OK-suh-juhn) an invisible gas found in water or air that people and animals need to breathe

pigment (PIG-muhnt) a substance that gives color to something

prism (PRIZ-uhm) a triangular object that separates white light into a spectrum of colors

variables (VAIR-ee-uh-buhlz) factors or conditions that can be changed in some way to produce meaningful outcomes in an experiment

For More Information

BOOKS

Baumann, Anne-Sophie. *The Ultimate Book of Planet Earth*. San Francisco: Chronicle Books, 2019.

Markovics, Joyce. *Carnivorous Plants*. Ann Arbor, MI: Cherry Lake Publishing, 2021.

Planet Earth. New York: DK Publishing, 2022.

WEBSITES
Explore these online sources with an adult:

Britannica Kids: Plant

NASA Climate Kids: Plants

PBS Kids: Things That Grow—Plants and Trees

Index

About the Author

Susan H. Gray has a master's degree in zoology. She has written more than 100 science and reference books for children, and especially loves writing about biology. Susan also likes to garden and play the piano. She lives in Cabot, Arkansas, with her husband, Michael, and many pets.